JUDI WARREN

PRAIRIE PIONEER QUILTERS
of GRAND ISLAND, NEBRASKA

PRAIRIE PIONEER QUILTERS
of GRAND ISLAND, NEBRASKA

FABRIC POSTCARDS

LANDMARKS & LANDSCAPES · MONUMENTS & MEADOWS

American Quilter's Society

P. O. Box 3290 • Paducah, KY 42002-3290

Except where otherwise noted,
photography is by the author.

Cover and title page photos:
Fabric Postcard:
OMOTE-SANDŌ IN AUTUMN; TOKYO,
5½" x 7½", 1993. Judi Warren
Cover fabric: Marimekko®
Cover photo of author: Erin Kate Pauken

Warren, Judi.
    Fabric Postcards : landmarks & landscapes, monuments & meadows /
Judi Warren.
        p.   cm.
    Includes index.
    ISBN 0-89145-833-6 : $22.95
    1. Quilting-Patterns   2. Patchwork-Patterns.   3. Postcards in
art.   1. Title.
TT835.W373   1994
746.46-dc20   94-6509
                                                                   CIP

Additional copies of this book may be ordered from:

American Quilter's Society
P.O. Box 3290
Paducah, KY 42002-3290
@$22.95. Add $1.00 for postage and handling.

For my grandmother
Emma Adella Pike

and

my granddaughter
Emma Austin Pauken

TABLE OF CONTENTS

FOREWORD

The true teacher draws from her students the best and the most of which they are capable. She exposes the students' talents and insights, and creates an atmosphere so positive and supportive that the student feels no fear – only exhilaration. It is rare to find such a gifted teacher, and Judi Warren is one.

This unique talent for awakening creative impulses has combined in Judi's teaching with a singular vehicle for this expression: fabric postcards.

While viewing thousands of quilts through years of teaching, judging, and participating in California's state quilt search, I have become aware of specific qualities or aspects of a quilt that always demand attention. When we encounter them, they fire a response because we sense the individual within the quilt. In such quilts, the quiltmakers have revealed themselves in their work in such a way that we come to know them, and may become aware of their likes and dislikes, their vulnerabilities, their determination, their intrepid spirit, their passions, their frugal nature, or their willingness to flaunt the conventions of their time to do what they consider important. Perfection, convention, and technique, nice as they may be, pale beside revelations of individuality and expressiveness. These are the quilts we remember – the ones with spirit and singularity, the ones that reveal, that tell us something of the lives of their makers.

Judi has offered her students a perfect means for bringing their own stories into existence through fabric. Postcards are steeped in memory, emotion, and history – contents which make them vital, exciting, funny or sad, nostalgic or philosophic.

With this book a door opens through which quilters can readily venture forth to reveal their own past experiences or encounters with the spirits of distant places and other times. They can step tentatively through the door, feeling their way carefully and protectively. Or they

by Jean Ray Laury

can plunge through to encounter everything headlong, face to face. Each proceeds with his or her own degree of caution or tosses caution to the wind. Either way, the work that evolves will be personal, open, and revealing. It will be as exciting and satisfying for the viewer as for the postcard-maker/artist.

Reading and working with this book is a pleasure. Judi has clarified many complex aspects of composition. She is constantly opening our minds to alternatives and expanding the possibilities. Within that framework of openness, she defines the steps which make the process so simple and satisfying.

That so many of Judi's students have shared their work attests to the strength and joy of the process as well as to their pleasure in the finished product. Totally absorbed by these works, I have become inspired to start sewing cards of my own.

One of the greatest pleasures in the "quilt world" has been the opportunity to know quilters everywhere, including many teachers. Few offer the charm, the wisdom, the mischievous delight, and the total faith in her students that Judi does. Her wit and warmth are evident in her postcards, and her ability to inspire is apparent in her students' interpretations. We are fortunate when we have her present – and when we don't, it is our good fortune to now have this book for guidance.

Thank you, Judi. You have expanded our lives, enlivened our work, and made sewing both more meaningful and more fun.

January 1994

WITH THANKS

Writing a book is a lot like making a quilt. Sentences and paragraphs, like pieces of cloth, are assembled and removed and reassembled; ideas wake you up in the middle of the night or distract you while you are standing in line at the Post Office. Although no one has ever had to force me to start a new quilt, I've discovered that a book doesn't get written without help and encouragement.

Much of that encouragement came from my husband, Ralph Warren. It was also generously given by Marty Bowne and Mary Lou Schwinn – who first suggested that the Fabric Postcards theme might make a nice book...by Meredith Schroeder of the American Quilter's Society – who agreed to make it happen...by Victoria Faoro, Executive Editor of AQS – who maintained limitless good humor and patience with a first-time author.

My thanks to Ann Bird, Nancy Crow, Nancy Halpern, Ikuko Kobayashi, Penny McMorris, Jean Wells, and others who shared opinions and advice, and most especially to Jean Ray Laury – a kind and gracious friend who gave me the benefit of her experience and insight.

I appreciate the cooperation and assistance of Atsuko Hashiura, Director of Hearts and Hands Patchwork Quilt School in Tokyo...Machiko Miyatani and Miwako Suzuki, who sent the Japanese students' Fabric Postcards to Maumee for photographing...not once, but twice! – and who answered my questions with unfailing patience and grace...my friends Rieko Ishii and Mariko Akizuki, whose knowledge of quiltmaking and fluency in both English and Japanese made it possible for me to teach the Fabric Postcards workshop in Osaka and Tokyo.

AND APPRECIATION

It is a pleasure to be able to include the work of Helen Bitar, Sue Broenkow, and Elly Sienkiewicz, as well as the Celestine Bacheller quilt from the collection of the Boston Museum of Fine Arts. We are indebted to unidentified makers of rubber stamps whose images provided a combination of playfulness and authenticity on the backs of the Fabric Postcards, and to all of the makers of both commercial and custom fabrics, whose textiles have given color and content to the picture side!

And, most especially, we recognize the contribution of the photographers and producers of the antique and contemporary postcards reproduced throughout the book; we regret that some of them could not be given full and complete credit because no current reference information was available. Nevertheless, their images are a valued educational resource that not only helped inspire the work that was accomplished, but also provided a basis for discussing design decisions and defining the visual relationships linking the fabric version to the source of inspiration.

Finally, to the participants in the Fabric Postcards Workshops – in Japan, at Point Bonita Quilter's Retreat, and at Quilt San Diego – go my thanks and abiding appreciation for work that embodies energy, enthusiasm, and expressiveness. Their efforts came from the heart, warmed MY heart, and exceeded my expectations.

Judi Warren   *January 1994*

Antique postcard.

PREFACE

The world has become very small.

Television brings us history as it happens. Fax machines send messages of great and small import across an ocean or a continent in the flash of a second. Telephone answering machines allow us to convey information or tell a joke to someone who isn't even there when we call.

Yet even in this high-tech world, the humble picture postcard continues to serve as a vehicle for communication. When we find ourselves in a new and fascinating place and want to share the experience with a friend, we still send a picture – of a conservatory or a quilt, a canyon or a cathedral – with the almost universal message inscribed or implied:

"…wish you were here."

In this book, you will find a Japanese quiltmaker's memory of Barcelona, Spain, and another's view of the Manhattan skyline at night…one Californian's remembrance of the English countryside and another's interpretation of the Eiffel Tower…as well as other vacation memories and jokes between friends. These fabric creations are in every sense picture postcards, complete in every detail to the real thing…except that they are executed in cloth.

Whether you are a quiltmaker or a traveler (or both), or simply someone who loves the appeal of color and pattern and the feel of fabric, I hope you will enjoy seeing the results of these efforts to capture a place, a time, an event – and that these fabric post-cards will encourage you to make one of your own, finding inspiration in the world around you.

TRIP AROUND THE WORLD:
An Introduction

We live in a time when many people travel to more places in one year than their own grandparents did in their lifetimes. Family vacations that involve driving from Boston to San Diego, and back home again are not uncommon. Airlines offer weekend trips to Paris. Business travelers leave home in the morning, fly to a meeting in another city, and are back home in time for dinner that same evening.

FIG. 1-1. DIXIE SIGHTSEEING ON LOOKOUT MOUNTAIN, 17" X 20½", 1989. Judi Warren. Collection: Dr. Dawn Glanz; Bowling Green, Ohio. Photo: Jeffrey Stewart.

In the world of quiltmaking, as in many other fields, traveling teachers and students have opportunities to visit and work in places they never dreamed of seeing. They go to conferences, symposiums, and exhibitions across a state or across the world, seeing new sights, meeting new friends, and sending postcards to old friends back home.

It was my own fascination with antique postcards that provided the impetus for making fabric postcards. In 1988, I had begun experimenting with a series of fabric triptychs in which antique postcards were superimposed on pieced fabric surfaces, a process that continues to intrigue me. Initially, my use of postcards only involved placing them as collage elements within the fabric compositions. However, it soon became more of a challenge to expand the image that stopped at the edge of the paper postcard, extending it into the surrounding fabric – so that a paper river could flow into a cloth river and a single blossom become a garden. That process suggested the idea of *making* postcards with fabric, rather than just *adding* paper postcards to pieced fabric surfaces.

FIG. 1-2. Detail: DIXIE SIGHTSEEING ON LOOKOUT MOUNTAIN.

Fabric postcards employ basic piecing and appliqué techniques no different than those used in making a quilt of larger size. They have relationships to many aspects of quilt design – or any other kind of two-dimensional design. In my classes and workshops, a primary goal has been to encourage quiltmakers to find ways of adding to the heritage rather than merely repeating it. I have always thought that the most eloquent quilts from the traditional past were the ones *about something*, the ones that had great personal meaning for the quiltmaker. So, in presenting the idea of fabric postcards in a classroom setting, each student is asked to draw upon experience and memory to define the content of a place they love.

Because it is a process that in most instances has involved plotting the elements of an already-existing composition, making a fabric postcard focuses attention on visual relationships, the vocabulary of the principles of design, and the real character and properties of color. In using cloth as a medium to record the world, equal portions of intuition and theory are called into play as the maker responds to the picture on the postcard – looking at small bits of fabric with an eye toward the pictorial information they might contain; understanding, for example, that a fabric which in any other pieced environment would simply be a floral print can *become* a garden or a meadow of thistles. Or that geometric prints can *become* the bark of a tree, the trestle of a bridge, city lights, or shadowed doorways.

There is no "kit" and there are no already-answered questions – there are only questions to be answered. Within the creative context of a fabric postcard there is also exploration and discovery, making the postcard an ideal format for stimulating creativity and inventive problem solving.

TRADITION REVISITED: Parallels in Quiltmaking

Themes inspired by geography, nature, and travel have often influenced the content of both pieced and appliquéd bed covers and wall quilts. Evidence of that influence is found not only in the design composition of geometric and pictorial blocks, but also in quilt titles like North Carolina Lily and New York Beauty, which read like an atlas or a visual diary. Recording the same terrain and natural phenomena that are the subject matter for modern-day picture postcards, Lady of the Lake and Delectable Mountains defined geographical features of the landscape, and Storm at Sea and Ocean Waves were natural events transformed into pieced geometric compositions. We can also find in traditional quilts a more specific record of traveling through the landscape – a history, in fact, of the crossing of a continent.

The westward migration of the 1800's was, of course, a very different proposition from a family camping trip involving visits to ten national parks on the way to Disneyland! The westward movement was not about taking a vacation; it was about moving. It was about leaving a place that you loved, probably forever, and if you succeeded in reaching your destination, establishing a new life under the most difficult of circumstances in an unfamiliar and sometimes hostile locale.

Generations of pioneers who participated in the expansion of the American frontier also made quilts. They made quilts not only about the homes they left behind, but also about the rivers, mountains, and prairies they passed on their way west. And they often gave those quilts titles that described the hardships and the optimism of what they were experiencing – names like Rocky Road to Kansas and Road to California. They recorded their travels in cloth rather than by means of a postcard's photograph depicting Route 66, the Northern Lights, or a desert in full bloom.

Baltimore Album quilts often contained blocks in which renderings of public buildings, historical monuments, and significant architectural sites were present – themes also found in contemporary postcards depicting, for example, the White House, the Chrysler Building, or the St. Louis Arch. Another example of the parallels between typical postcard imagery and both classic and more recent quilts is Elly Sienkiewicz's Statue of Liberty block titled Yearning to Breathe Free (Fig. 2-1). It reflects the influence of the Baltimore Album style and uses an image that is recognized the world over.

FIG. 2-1. YEARNING TO BREATHE FREE, 12½" x 12½", 1987. Elly Sienkiewicz (cotton, silk, ink, acrylic paint). Photo: Sharon Risedorph.

Countless groups of quiltmakers have presented their communities with celebratory quilts made with commemorative blocks picturing the band shell in the city park, the fountain in the town square, historical homes, and municipal buildings – the scenery and architecture of beloved "home towns." One of the most heartfelt and appealing quilts about a home town may be one made by Celestine Bacheller, who used silk, velvet, and multicolored embroidery to document houses, gardens, and views of the sea in her quilt about Wyoma, Massachusetts (Fig. 2-2).

A miniature fabric landscape or building-scape in a postcard format is not far removed from the content or intent of many traditional quilt themes; making one can challenge your creativity, heighten your fluency with design concepts, and expand your ability to translate visual information to the same extent as does the designing of any quilt. It will be a pictorially-expressed "trip around the world" that speaks of familiar places, new

FIG. 2-2.CRAZY QUILT, 74¼" x 57", 1850 - 1900. Celestine Bacheller (pieced, appliquéd, and embroidered silk and velvet). Gift of Mr. and Mrs. Edward J. Healy in memory of Mrs. Charles O'Malley. Courtesy of the Museum of Fine Arts, Boston, MA.

vistas, and memorable times on a smaller and more intimate scale than a full-size quilt and that, happily, will require hours – not months – to complete.

FORMATS:
Scenic Views and
Multiple Images

Fabric postcards can simply be thought of as very tiny quilts, as beautiful small cloth objects that you can hold in your hand rather than sleep under. They may take the form of a personal memento – a little present to yourself – in which you express your most poignant memory of an unforgettable time or place, your favorite city in the world, the sun rising behind the Golden Gate Bridge, or even your own garden at the height of the blooming season.

Perhaps one of the most appropriate uses of a fabric postcard parallels that of an acutal postcard – as a gift to express a special "thank you" to a dear friend, to commemorate the shared experience of an evening boat ride around the tip of Manhattan, or a walk beside the sea at Cape Hattaras. When the fabric postcard is a gift, it may be hand-delivered or actually sent through the mail in a protective transparent envelope. (If you're not too nervous, you might even mail it unprotected with a real stamp sewn on, to be hand-cancelled at the post office.)

A fabric postcard need not be thought of as a single cloth memento; you may discover that making one will lead you to want to make more! If you want to combine several within a single composition, there are various options that you might consider. For instance, a collection of images based on a common theme might be developed as little vignettes placed randomly on a larger ground. Of course, a series of fabric postcards can also be arranged in rows of thematically-related blocks in a kind of landscape or architecture sampler quilt. In Helen Bitar's quilt (Fig. 3-1, right), the subject matter stays the same throughout, yet the composition and colors change in subtle ways from block to block. As each block has its own unique expressiveness and character, this quilt is a lovely example of variations within a theme inspired by a landscape!

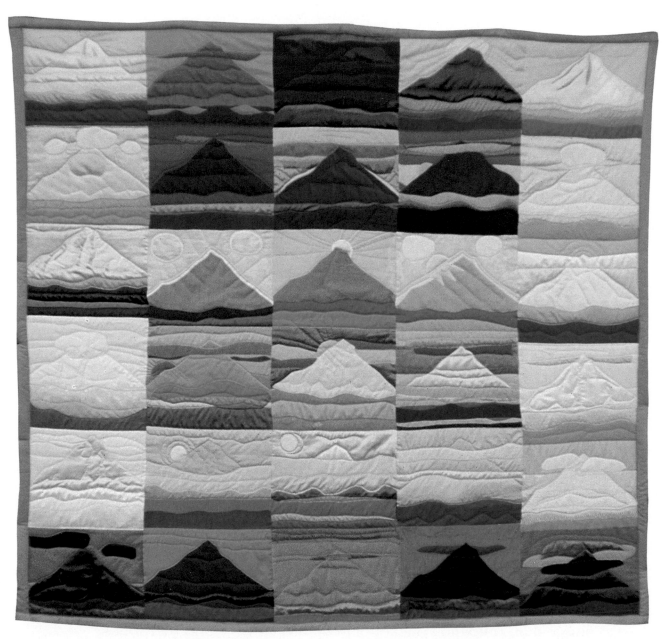

Fig. 3-1. THE MOUNTAIN FROM MY WINDOW, 98" x 92", 1975. Helen Bitar. Collection: Robert Pfannebecker;
Lancaster, PA. Photo: Helen Bitar.

Another approach for introducing multiples of an image into a larger composition is demonstrated in Sue Broenkow's quilt called "Redhead in a Blanket" (Fig. 3-2). Here, pieced mountain-scape blocks have been mirrored and arranged edge to edge to create a larger landscape and a more distant vista.

Fig. 3-2. REDHEAD IN A BLANKET, 55" x 34", 1992. Sue Broenkow. Photo: Valerie Schmidt-Wilson.

While the preceding examples suggest ways to use postcard-like subjects in quilt-like formats, it is also possible to work more specifically with the concept of postcards themselves, by focusing on the way we might see them displayed on the rack in the store where they are sold.

For example, the following postcard panels illustrating five views of Tokyo and five views of Kyoto are based on photographs taken in Japan. The top postcard in each of the panels shown in Fig. 3-3 is sewn to a fabric envelope shape reminiscent of a mailing package; the individual pictures (each 5½" x 7½") are joined together by hand, angled to suggest an unfolding packet of postcard views – and memories.

The fabrics were chosen to reflect as faithfully as possible the contents, colors, textures, and patterns in the photos. You will note, though, that while some of these fabric postcards are very faithful to the composition of the photographs, others are merely loosely inspired by the general theme (Figs. 3-4a – 3-13b).

FIG. 3-3. TOKYO POSTCARDS/KYOTO POSTCARDS, 31¾" x 7½", 1990. Judi Warren. Machine pieced/hand appliquéd.

Fig. 3-4a. Plastic flower wreath; Shinjuku-ku, Tokyo.

Fig. 3-4b. The vivid flowers in the fabric echo the intensity of the plastic blossoms.

Fig. 3-5a. A rainy night in the shop area at Asakusa Temple, Tokyo.

Fig. 3-5b. The fabric version focuses on the upper left half of the photo image, highlighting the white plastic decorations against the night sky.

Fig. 3-6a. Obentō (Japanese lunch boxes) in a shop window display.

Fig. 3-6b. The fabric lunch is only "fish" and "rice."

FABRIC POSTCARDS

Fig. 3-7a. Courtyard with snow and leaves.

Fig. 3-7b. Meiji Shrine, Tokyo.

Fig. 3-8a. Facade of the
Miyazaki building in Tokyo.

Fig. 3-8b. At the top of the stairs is Hearts and Hands Patchwork Quilt School, where
there is always a quilt in the window.

Fig. 3-9a. A fascinating wall
on the grounds of Toji Temple
in Kyoto.

Fig. 3-9b. The fabrics focus on the architectural details.

Fig. 3-10a. Street sign, corner of Oike Dôri and Kawaramachi Dôri, Kyoto.

Fig. 3-10b. Fabric rendering of the sign.

Fig. 3-11a. Brooms and brushes in a Kyoto shop window.

Fig. 3-11b. The fringed silk fabric expresses the brush bristles; the numbers stamped on a remnant of old kimono fabric are the code numbers on the brushes.

Fig. 3-12a. Garlands of origami cranes at Fushimi Inari, Kyoto.

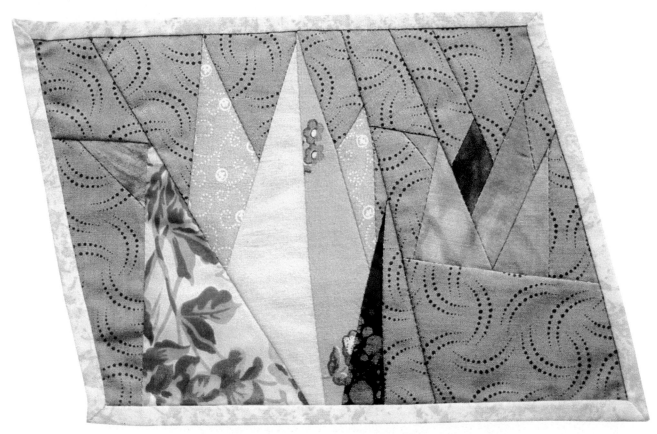

Fig. 3-12b. Pieced origami cranes.

Fig. 3-13a. Red-orange torii
gates at Fushimi Inari.

Fig. 3-13b. The height of the gates is diminished in this horizontal composition, but the
intensity of their color is maintained.

The preceding examples suggest how postcard fronts can be interpreted in fabric. Still another approach might be to concentrate attention on the message side of a postcard, rather than the picture side – so that the *back* of a postcard becomes the *front* of the quilt! The piece below (Fig. 3-14) was made in celebration of the tenth anniversary of The Hearts and Hands Quilt Festival in Tokyo. It contains all the elements you would expect to see on the back of a postcard, and its size allows for focusing on such details as the stamp, postmark, cancellation mark, address, and message. Some of the words are written in indelible ink; others are quilted, pieced, and appliquéd.

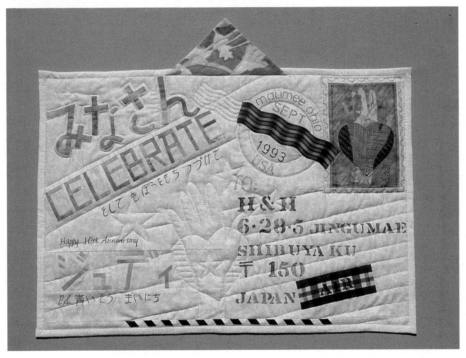

Fig. 3-15. Detail: EVERYBODY CELEBRATE, (above). Appliquéd and pieced lettering.

Fig. 3-14. EVERYBODY CELEBRATE, 23" x 27", 1993. Judi Warren. Collection of Hearts and Hands Patchwork Quilt School; Tokyo, Japan.

Fig. 3-16. Detail: EVERYBODY CELEBRATE, (above). The parallel curves in this Pilgrim/Roy fabric describe perfectly the lines in a cancellation mark.

Most of the fabric postcards in this book are pictorial; they are literal and faithful renditions of a photographic source. In fact, abstract compositions, crazy-pieced surfaces, and other non-pictorial designs done in postcard dimensions can offer still other possibilities for exploration! However, while there are many ways that the postcard theme can inspire ideas to be interpreted in cloth, most often it is the picture on the front – and the memories that picture stirs – that are the motivating force.

LANDMARKS & LANDSCAPES: Potential Themes

Whether you're planning to work from a photographic source or to develop an "invented" postcard based on memory, there are several themes from which to choose. However, you will discover that some will be less appropriate than others. For example, herds of animals and crowd scenes will probably be unsatisfactory and difficult to achieve – as you can see from the example below. Ultimately, landscape and architecture seem to offer the most advantageous imagery and the best chance for a happy outcome!

Bathing Ghat, Howrah Bridge.

Fig. 4-1. Antique postcard.

Fig. 4-2. Antique postcard.

Fig. 4-3. Antique postcard.

NEW POST OFFICE AND FEDERAL BUILDING, LOS ANGELES, CAL.

Fig. 4-4. Antique postcard.

Fabric postcard landscapes may be inspired by travel diaries and family vacations or by dream trips and imaginary journeys; by places as far away as the other side of the world or as close as your own backyard. What is important is that you have a personal affinity for that place.

If you're more intrigued by architectural subject matter, you might start with a postcard view of your favorite building – the facade of an Art Deco hotel in Miami or the Tower of London, a movie theater or a Mayan Temple. On a more personal level, you might build a whole collection of fabric postcards that depict several buildings significant in your life, such as your elementary school, the place where you first worked, the place where you were married, your own home, or your grandparents' home.

There is a nice relationship between architectural themes and traditional House and School House quilt blocks; however, geographical and natural themes also offer a myriad of potential subjects. A love of nature and a respect for the environment can be expressed through real and imaginary views of deserts, mountain ranges, jungles, meadows – or the jellyfish display at the Monterey Bay Aquarium. The list is endless!

COMPOSTION & CONTENT: Designing a Fabric Postcard

The appeal of a fabric postcard lies in its simplicity and its smallness. Making a postcard involves the challenge of faithfully reproducing a specific image in as much detail as possible, using an economy of means within a limited size. However, it is not simply a process involving the duplication of an already-existing image. An understanding of both the image and the content it reflects are very important. Personal insights enable you to express that specific image directly and simply in cloth.

The primary reason for making a fabric postcard is to create a beautiful and personally satisfying object that records a place that you love. In order to accomplish a well-executed fabric postcard, you will need to consider the same visual questions that you address in any design problem-solving situation. In order for your card to be as eloquent as possible, you will proceed through a sequence of looking, *really* seeing, and sometimes eliminating.

Interpreting and selecting are very important, in much the same way as they are for art students studying and replicating the works of the masters in order to grasp working procedures and gain deeper understanding. In making fabric postcards, interpreting and selecting become all the more important because in small-scale pieces you want to use the fewest number of fabrics possible to say as much as possible. Each decision becomes crucial.

The experience of making a fabric postcard will certainly motivate you to look less casually when selecting fabrics for any piece, large or small, and you may also discover that it generates new approaches to the designing of original quilts. But it is important to remember that the uniqueness of a fabric postcard lies in its inner relationships of size, scale, pattern, and composition. It is a mistake to assume that the fabrics or composition of a successful 5½" x 8½" fabric postcard would be equally successful enlarged to 5½' x 8½'. For example, my fabric postcard depicting the red-orange torii gates at Fushimi Inari (p. 31) would be dreadful were it arbitrarily enlarged to 6' by 7'!

You need to be realistic about the amount of visual information a postcard-sized format can support. It would be futile to attempt to reduce the quilt pictured below (Fig. 5-1) to postcard dimensions with every detail intact!

FIG. 5-1. MARCH 28, 1986: RAIN AT FUSHIMI INARI, 88" X 72", 1988. Judi Warren. Photo: Brian Blauser.

FIG. 5-2. TORII GATES, 16½" x 17", 1986. Judi Warren. Collection: Keiko Takahashi; Kyoto, Japan.

Similarly, even the small wallhanging above (Fig. 5-2) probably contains more detail than you could successfully include in a postcard.

Awareness of the visual elements in a photo source will help you set realistic goals for your fabric postcard, and help you select fabrics whose style, character, coloration, pattern, and scale will best express the content of the image. Remember: you are not trying to re-create all the subtleties of a photograph; you are making a small fabric image that uses elements of the photograph as a jumping-off place leading to something that has its own unique qualities. Of course you will want to satisfy yourself that you can gather fabrics that are as faithful as possible to the colors, the kinds and intensities of colors, the values, and the value relationships found in the photo source – as with a larger quilt, by trying out various combinations until you are pleased with what you see.

Specifically, you will want to consider the following visual elements:

•In most instances, you will be working from a photo source that will provide a proto-type of the *composition* and layout, as well as offer clues to understanding the proportional relationships within the photo image and the translating of those relationships into a larger format.

•In developing your composition, you may find it necessary to *simplify*. You'll want to be realistic about the limitations of working on a miniature scale, choosing the most crucial details and rejecting unnecessary ones without diminishing the impact of the final result. While your fabric postcard will undoubtedly be larger than your photo source, you are making a post*card* and not a post*er*!

•In order to avoid making hasty decisions about the choice of fabrics, you will need to study the photo source in order to search out the most expressive fabric to show the *coloration* of a mountain in the distance or the subtleties of a wheat field.

•Another important consideration will involve *values* and *value contrasts*. Again, the photo source will provide a guide as to how much darker the values in a mountain are than the values in a meadow.

•You'll also want to give attention to the *scale* of patterned fabrics as they relate to both the visual details of the photo source and to the dimensions of the fabric version.

•As with any other textile piece, *craftmanship* will be a vital ingredient, not only because of the small-scale nature of what you are attempting, but more importantly because you'll want to achieve the clean, crisp, flat quality of a paper card. Although you may need to use a minimal amount of embroidery to express small details that cannot be done any other way, fabric postcards are most effective when you express your idea via a minimum number of carefully selected fabrics pieced and/or appliquéd as cleanly as possible, rather than relying on heavily-applied embellishments.

•It is, however, the visual *content* of the fabrics you use that will have the greatest impact on the eloquence of your fabric postcard. Choosing them will involve your looking at fabrics from a different viewpoint than if you were choosing them for a wall or bed quilt. After you have familiarized yourself with the visual characteristics of the imagery in the photo source, fabrics can be gathered and chosen based on their patterns, textures, style, character, and personality – qualities which will achieve a balance between a desire for strict duplication and the pure enjoyment of the fabrics for their own unique qualities in combination with each other. Your search will be more for essence than for photo-realism.

A photo source may be an antique or contemporary postcard or it may be a favorite photograph you have taken yourself. Of course, there is an advantage in working from your own photography in that you will have already "composed" the image when you took the picture. If you plan to make fabric postcards for any purpose other than as individual personal mementos, it is preferable to find inspiration in your own photographs so that the whole process originates with you.

Once you have chosen your subject, based on an association or a memory or simply because you are intrigued by the challenge of the imagery, you'll be ready to begin gathering fabrics. In searching for the essence that is a combination of personal memory, invention, and adherence to the photo image, you will want to try out several fabrics to arrive at the most expressive choices for each major area of the composition. You will want to think not only about what is the best choice for each major element in the image, but also the effect that these fabrics will have on each other.

We can assume that several elements will be important parts of a fabric postcard, no matter what the theme. In almost every fabric postcard there will be a horizon line and therefore a need for a fabric that functions for sky. You'll find various solutions in the works illustrated in this book. Sky fabrics are often the easiest to find. Below (Fig. 5-3) are some examples that suggest the idea of sky through a quality of some degree of atmospheric pattern of light. You are also likely to need to look for patterns and colorations that will express natural elements and architectural textures (Figs. 5-4, 5-5, 5-6).

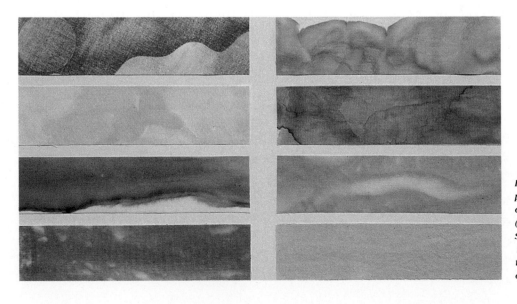

FIG. 5-3. The subtle cloud-like patterning found in custom-dyed and hand-painted fabrics (available from sources such as Shades, Inc. and Skydyes, p. 119) seem more naturalistic than solids, which have a flatter appearance.

FIG. 5-4 . Foliage-like patterns express lawns, meadows, shrubs, and treetops.

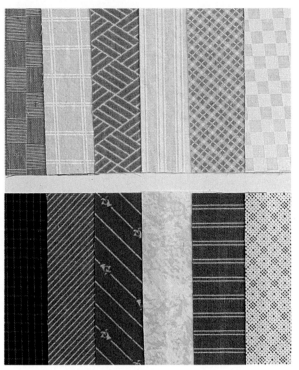

FIG. 5-5 . Architectural surfaces might be expressed by fabrics similar to these examples.

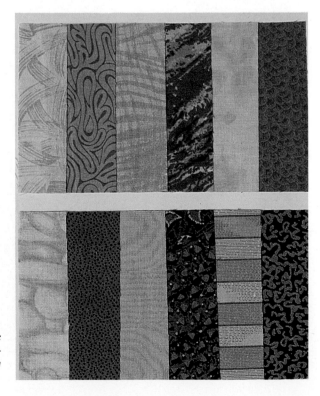

FIG. 5-6 (right). Fabrics such as these suggest the textural qualities of marble, wood, stone, or concrete and that might also work well for paving blocks, gravel paths, and city sidewalks.

If you're lucky, a single piece of fabric will contain many areas of color and textural pattern that seem to be made-to-order for your needs. For example, the stair steps in the Fairmont Hotel postcard (Fig. 5-7, below) could be stated nicely via the black/rust line pattern in the fabric shown. The addition of a few more fabrics carefully chosen so their value, intensity, scale, and other properties reflect details of both color and content will get you started.

The Albion, Michigan, postcard (Fig. 5-8, right) depicting a quiet afternoon on a small-town residential street will require fabrics that work expressively for the context of green lawns, treetops, sidewalks, wood frame houses, rooftops, flower beds in front of the porch railing, flowers on the trellis – and that will suggest the kinds of color and value relationships found in the antique postcard source. The key to choosing fabrics for your fabric postcard is in doing so not by making hasty choices and assumptions, but by *looking* carefully at both the card and the cloth and *seeing* that a tree's trunk is not merely brown – it is also taupe and violet and gray – or that a sky is not merely blue but rather is white plus several tints of blue and pink.

FIG. 5-7. Fabrics for the Fairmont Hotel.

FIG. 5-8. Michigan Avenue postcard and fabrics.

While pictorial, even the most literal of patterned fabrics – fabrics in which we can iden-tify leaves or distinguish daisies from lilacs – are not photo-realistic. They are stylized designs. While it is challenging to look for fabrics that do exactly what the photo source does, it would be miraculous to actually find them! Sometimes, a particular fabric's color and value will be perfect, but the scale of the pattern will be too big – or the scale will be just right but the color will not. All that is important is that you gather fabrics that for the most part echo the colors, values, textures, and scale needed and that you find them pleasing in close proximity to each other! In other words, it is fine to just enjoy the fabrics for themselves. Even though you may have both literal and abstract prints from which to choose, you will find that scale and coloration may influence your final choice more than pictorial accuracy.

Below (Fig. 5-9) is an old postcard view of a lake at Allen Park in Augusta, Georgia. In the experimental mock-up inspired by this postcard (Fig. 5-10, right), you will see that some of the pictorial elements have been stated as mere abstract suggestions. A portion of the water-lilies had to become tulips – the color and scale of this fabric are reasonably accurate, and I could find no water lily fabric that worked as well!

A decision was also made to depart a little from making a literal picture and use a swatch of abstract floral drapery fabric in which little orange shapes only suggest the orange color of the roof tops on the houses behind the lake. The reflection of the trees in the water was achieved by using both the back and the front sides of one fabric. An uneven sliver of "foliage" fabric stretching across the horizontal line would complete the picture.

In the size of the fabric mock-up (5¼" x 8¼") these particular fabrics loosely express the mood of a specific landscape; the scale of their patterns is compatible with the dimensions of the piece. But it is a false assumption to think that since these fabrics work in this size they would be equally appropriate if the image were enlarged to 5' x 8'. Enlarging the design with no attempt to replace each piece of fabric with a larger-scale print would only result in a piece that has increased in size but lost all its charm and

LAKE IN ALLEN PARK, AUGUSTA, GA.

FIG. 5-9. Postcard source.

intimacy. The piece would become flat and awkward and lifeless! A large pictorial quilt presents different problems and requires entirely different solutions. A fabric postcard has its own functions and reasons.

FIG. 5-10. Experimental fabric mock-up; Lake at Allen Park.

FIG. 5-11. Although the little fabric house (above) might seem to be ideal, it also seems too cartoon-like among the other fabrics.

THE PICTORIAL IMAGE: Making a Fabric Postcard

Since this book is not about basic piecing and appliqué methods, but about looking and translating personal themes into cloth images, the following pages will suggest working procedures relating to both the looking and the translating. You'll be able to think more specifically about design and composition once you have satisfied yourself that you have gathered fabrics that will express the mood you are seeking. It is helpful

Fig. 6-1. The fashion center of Tokyo, Omote-Sandō in Autumn. (Contemporary postcard.)

to start with a tentative mock-up in an experimental combination of fabrics. In the preliminary example below (Fig. 6-2), certain details from the Omote-Sandō postcard (Fig. 6-1) have already been eliminated – i.e. the traffic, the parked cars, the street signs, and the lampposts.

Fig. 6-2. Experimental fabric mock-up.

Removing these details gives the opportunity to refine the composition and to emphasize the mysterious blue-violet light between the tree branches, to make the fabric version more atmospheric and colorful. The speckled fabric seemed to express an abstraction of tree bark texture and to produce the effect of little flecks of sunlight.

At this point, a compositional line-drawing diagram which is larger than the actual postcard will help you decide on dimensions and to finalize the design composition (Fig. 6-3).

Fig. 6-3. Line drawing traced from an enlargement of the Omote-Sandō postcard.

In the 5¼" x 7¼" finished version (see cover and title page), the colors changed slightly from those in the experimental mock-up. Although cut from the same fabrics, the final choices were selected from different areas of those fabrics. The tree trunks were appliquéd; the branches were backed with an iron-on facing cut into slivers and appliquéd "raw" to suggest a twig-like appearance.

The following illustrations explore a sequence of working methods for a fabric version inspired by the Central Park; Pasadena, California, postcard (Fig. 6-4). Getting started involves looking closely at the photo source for compositional clues and gathering fabrics that will express each area of the composition. First, by enlarging the photo source on a photocopy machine, you can maintain the integrity of the proportions of the interior relationships and you'll also be able to experiment with a range of sizes until you find one that is realistic in terms of the degree of detail you wish to accomplish versus the limitations that the fabrics and the sewing processes may impose. Generally, you'll want something in the range of 6" x 9" (slightly larger or smaller). This photocopy-machine enlargement will also serve as a guide for accurate attention to the value relationships.

FLOWERS AND PALMS AT CENTRAL PARK, PASADENA, CAL.

Fig. 6-4 (left). Antique postcard.

Fig. 6-5 (below). Black and white photocopy enlargement of Central Park postcard.

FLOWERS AND PALMS AT CENTRAL PARK, PASADENA, CAL.

Tracing paper laid over that enlarged copy will allow you to diagram the major forms, simplifying where necessary, and omitting elements you don't want to include. (The wispy tree in the distance, outlined by a dotted line in Fig. 6-6, will not be present in the final version.) The dotted lines at the left and right edges indicate parts of the composition that will be concealed by the binding. The tracing paper overlay will also serve as an aid for making templates for pieced and appliquéd shapes (Fig. 6-7).

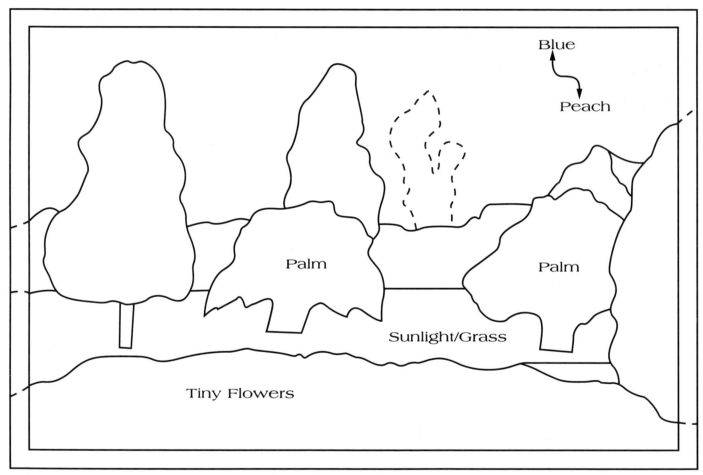

Fig. 6-6.

Further study of the photo source, the enlarged copy, and the diagram will be helpful both in selecting fabrics and in determining construction methods. In choosing fabrics for pictorial content, there will always be "good" choices and "better" choices, so it really helps to see each potential fabric in position and in context with all the others in the composition – in order to assess which are best. It is a process of trial-and-error, of proposing and rejecting until you arrive at the most pleasing relationships. The following illustrations demonstrate some steps in the fabric selection process for making the Central Park fabric postcard.

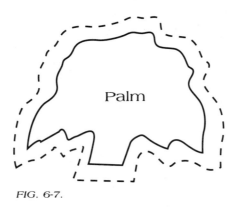

FIG. 6-7.

FIG. 6-8. Here, the tree at the left seems to lack depth.

FIG. 6-9. Now, the tree at the right seems incompatible with its neighbors.

FIG. 6-10. The foliage fabric is perfect for the tree at the right, but the value is much too dark.

FIG. 6-11. Again, the right-hand tree is still too dark in value. Using one fabric for the foreground flower bed does not work as well as two different florals.

FIG. 6-12. Now the tree at the right looks like "green sky" – it is too atmospheric.

FIG. 6-13. The two fabrics in the right-hand tree have too high a contrast of value and the giant strawberry seems out of place both in scale and in content.

Of course, the kinds of fabrics you choose will have some bearing on your choices of construction methods and sewing processes. Often, it works well to join a "sky" shape to a "land" shape to create a horizontal line on which you can build other elements. Another method is to build the entire image on a foundation fabric the size of the finished fabric postcard. This foundation cloth can be plain muslin which will be totally concealed as the image is completed or it can be a fabric that will be left visible in certain areas so that it becomes a design element.

In the final version of the Central Park postcard (Fig. 6-14, right), a foliage-fabric horizontal line was hand-appliquéd to the sky shape; then the foreground was stitched on by machine. While you will be working most often with appliqué and machine or hand piecing, you may need to consider minimal use of fabric collage using an iron-on facing for small details that are too tiny to be stated any other way. You may also want to add tiny touches of drawing or embroidery, while remembering that heavily applied beads and sequins will not contribute to the flat and crisp quality you are seeking!

FIG. 6-14. Fabric postcard: FLOWERS AND PALMS AT CENTRAL PARK, 7¾" x 5½", 1991. Judi Warren.

WISH YOU WERE HERE: Quiltmakers' Fabric Postcards

The fabric postcards on pages 57 through 103 were made by quiltmakers from around the world and are about the whole world. They represent themes depicting seasides and coastlines of Yucatan, Florida, California, and Hawaii...landscapes inspired by meadows, city parks, and country fields...and architectural subjects including cathedrals, landmarks, monuments, temples, quiet streets, and glittering skylines.

Beneath the postcard or snapshot that was the inspiration, you will find an explanatory statement from each quiltmaker; on the opposite page is the fabric version, accompanied by brief comments summarizing design decisions, technical aspects, and the important visual relationships between the photo source and the cloth interpretation. The photographic source provides a framework for understanding which details were omitted, which were included, and the ways those details were translated in the fabric postcard.

As you leaf through the fabric postcards, you will notice that in several instances there is a balance between the use of specific representation and generality, that the scale of patterned cloth has been used both in accurate relationships and deliberately enlarged for exaggeration and emphasis, and that certain details can be omitted without diminishing the impact of the piece.

You may also notice that some of the photo sources have a little hole at the top, made by a push-pin or a thumb-tack that has held it to a wall or a bulletin board where its presence could be enjoyed (and felt) on a daily basis. In each fabric postcard there is a tangible emotional connection to an experience recalled – a memory defined.

FIG. 7. Yachiyo Monarrez, Los Angeles, California, 9¼" x 7¼". Collection: Anne Ito, Berkeley, CA.

The Inspiration

"This collage represents two wonderful days spent with my friend, Nesan Anne Ito. My artistic endeavor far lacks the quality of the time we had together. Just for the record, (for someone who detests driving) we clocked 300 miles just zipping around Pasadena, Montclair, and Costa Mesa – and enjoying tea at the Huntington Hartford Museum – with no care in the world."

Yachiyo Monarrez
Los Angeles, California

The Fabric Postcard

Yachiyo Monarrez did not work from any model or photographic guide, but only from the "pictures" in her own memory. Events are symbolized by details like the tea cups on a tiny table, streets of shops, and Yachiyo's dislike of driving (noted by an automobile caught in traffic, with a passenger and driver who look remarkably like Anne and Yachi!). This fabric postcard was a gift for a friend; it is a fabric diary that records experiences shared and enjoyed.

FIG. 7-1a. Photo, New York; skyline at night. Photo: Masatako Yamamoto.

The Picture/Postcard

"When my husband and I traveled to New York a few years ago, we enjoyed the sunset dinner cruises and the view of the Manhattan skyline."

Chikako Yamamoto
Osaka, Japan

FIG. 7-1b. Chikako Yamamoto, 8"x 5¾".

The Fabric Postcard

Chikako Yamamoto's beautifully crafted fabric postcard reveals what she saw from the deck of the cruise boat – the windows of the city are translated into columns of light glowing against the night sky, and there are tiny sparks of light reflected in the dark water. She achieved this effect with an interesting combination of plaids, abstract patterns, and botanical prints which become urban and architectural in the context of the postcard.

FIG. 7-2a. *"The Oakland Bay Bridge silhouetted by the early morning sun rising over beautiful San Francisco Bay." Postcard/Photo: John Wagner.*

The Picture/Postcard

"The Oakland/San Francisco area has always been a special place for my family. We lived there for three years and return for a visit every year. I used fabrics I bought at the Pacific International Quilt Festival in San Francisco, especially for Judi's workshop."

Barbara Friedman
San Diego, California

FIG. 7-2b. Barbara Friedman, 6¾" x 9⅜".

The Fabric Postcard

The startling yellow light in the original postcard's photograph becomes very abstract in Barbara Friedman's fabric version. Faithfully recording the varying intensities of the sky, while more loosely stating the shape of the yellow light dappling the surface of the water, she brings it all into focus via a Katie Pasquini-Masopust blue-and-black silk-screened fabric that very appropriately defines the structural grid of the Oakland Bay Bridge.

FIG. 7-3a. Yellow flowers; Hannya-ji; Nara, Japan. Postcard/photo: Takeshi Kanamoto.

The Picture/Postcard

"Hannya-ji is a very famous temple because of the many different kinds of flowers that bloom there each season. The autumn cosmos are the best flowers. I love the calm atmosphere and I visit often."

Sueko Itoh
Osaka, Japan

FIG. 7-3b. Sueko Itoh, 5½" x 7½".

The Fabric Postcard

The temple in Sueko Itoh's piece has such definition and clarity that we would recognize it as a temple building even without referring to the photographic source! While stating the clusters of foliage in a generalized way and only suggesting the delicate branch at the upper right edge, she has chosen fabrics having a very explicit relationship to the architectural details of the facade and the tiles of the roof.

FIG. 7-4a. "Christo: Surrounded Islands; 1980–1983. Biscayne Bay; Greater Miami, Florida." Post-card/Photo: Wolfgang Volz. ©Christo.

The Picture/Postcard

"I can't think of a better thing to do to Miami. (This well-worn post-card is a treasure I often carry with me.)"

Jeanne Creighton
Denver, Colorado

FIG. 7-4b. Jeanne Creighton, 9" x 6½".

The Fabric Postcard

Jeanne Creighton's sense of humor is evident in the brevity of her statement below her postcard, at left. On the reverse side of her fabric postcard is a fictional message from Christo himself, addressed to Jeanne in a mythical place called "Monochromatic, Colorado." She chose fabrics that emphasize the pattern and intense colors of the water and the pink island surroundings, making only casual reference to the city by means of an abstract print.

FIG. 7-5a. Park; Miyazaki City, Japan. Photo: Rumi Shikata.

The Picture/Postcard

"This is the park in Miyazaki City, where we lived for a few years. I was interested in showing the contrast between Pheonix (a tropical plant) and azalea (a Japanese plant)."

Rumi Shikata
Tokyo, Japan

FIG. 7-5b. Rumi Shikata, 7⅜" x 8⅜".

The Fabric Postcard

The fabric of Rumi Shikata's appliquéd palm tree is pictorially explicit – outlined against the sky exactly as it is in the photograph. In contrast, the mounds of bushes and blooming plants are translated into less specific shapes of color.

FIG. 7-6a. "Paris et ses Merveilles, Notre Dame (1163–1330)."
Book-plate catalog: Watercolor by Paul V. Delker.

The Picture/Postcard

"Notre Dame symbolizes my favorite city, but photographs seemed too complex to reproduce in a small format. In an old book-plate catalog, I found a simplified image and I chose fabrics for their architectural qualities. The message on the back recalls friends from student days in Paris."

Gail Retka Angiulo
Mill Valley, California

FIG. 7-6b. Gail Retka Angiulo, 6" x 8¾".

The Fabric Postcard

Carefully chosen fragments from patterned fabrics become mortared stones, Rose Windows, and pointed arches in Gail Retka Angiulo's Notre Dame fabric postcard. In contrast to the scale of the tiny checkered foreground fabric, the cathedral correctly assumes monumental proportions and is set against a gently modulated sky.

FIG. 7-12a. Isla Contoy Bird Sanctuary; Isla Mujeres, Yucatan. Photo: Neil Herring.

The Picture/Postcard

"The making of the fabric postcard was a true pleasure from start to finish. It produced immediate gratification and was a vacation experience in its own right."

Dena Bliss
California

FIG. 7-12b. Dena Bliss, 7⅝" x 5½".

The Fabric Postcard

Omitting the dock and the boat, Dena Bliss captured the expanse of sea and sky, the uninterrupted horizon and the freshness of the sunlight. There are only four crucially chosen fabrics in this clean and crisp fabric postcard, yet the card's little patch of beach, the delicately articulated palm trees, and the gentle modulations in the sky and water speak volumes!

RED ANTHURIUMS

FIG. 7-13a. "Red Anthuriums of the Kona Coast."

The Picture/Postcard

"I combined two postcards that I bought in Hawaii in the 1970's. A beautiful green Hoffman® print and some fabrics that I dyed years ago helped me choose which cards to interpret. I also had a wonderful fabric that looked like plumeria, a beautiful flower that grows in Hawaii. I faced this fabric with iron-on facing and cut out fourteen plumeria – to represent fourteen trips my husband and I had taken to the Islands."

Marie Goyette Fritz
San Diego, California

FIG. 7-13b. Marie Goyette Fritz, 8¼" x 6¼".

The Fabric Postcard

Rather than searching for fabrics that would satisfy the requirements of a specific postcard, Marie Goyette Fritz gathered her cloth first and then chose a postcard that could be expressed with those fabrics! The wreath of plumeria blossoms was inspired by the design of a second postcard picturing Waikiki Beach circled with a lei of flowers.

FIG. 7-14a. Lancaster County, Pennsylvania. Photo: Yoshi Nishimura.

The Picture/Postcard

"I traveled to Pennsylvania in the spring of 1990. We enjoyed the countryside for a long time while our tour bus was stopped by an accident on the road ahead."

Yoshi Nishimura
Kyoto, Japan

FIG. 7-14b. Yoshi Nishimura, 9⅛" x 6⅝".

The Fabric Postcard

While the descriptive sentence on the back of Yoshi Nishimura's fabric postcard says "The People's Place Quilt Museum," it is *really* a cloth picture of a Lancaster County farm she observed very closely during the time her tour bus was delayed by traffic *on the way to* the Museum! She was able to record very faithfully the buildings and the surrounding terrain. The fabric she used to define the raw earth of a field would be very elegant if used in a traditional block; combined with the pictorial elements of her postcard it becomes tilled soil.

FIG. 7-15a. "Salthouse, St. Nicholas Church, and Applewood Cottage."

The Picture/Postcard

"When our daughter was in England, she spent three years in the home of Janet and Colin Johnston – becoming not only a tenant, but also a member of the family. They shared their wonderful cottage at Salthouse, a small coastal village, with us. It is their much-loved retreat and it appears in the lower right-hand corner. This is a magical place and since many of their friends have painted this view, this is my contribution to their collection, as a thank you for their generosity and friendship."

Jill Prickett
Richmond, California

FIG. 7-15b. Jill Prickett, 8¾" x 7¾".

The Fabric Postcard

Jill Prickett describes this part of England as having "light that comes in swiftly shifting shadows" and "skies that seem to go on forever." Jill used fabrics that capture a softer, more silvery quality of light, which she feels is more characteristic of the skies in this region than the brilliant blue of the postcard. Her plaid cathedral evokes a suggestion of windows and architectural details; the horizontal direction in her water fabric becomes a placid sea.

FIG. 7-16a. Black Sands Beach, Hawaii. Photo: Andrew Bailey.

The Picture/Postcard

"In 1987, Andrew and I were on our 'paradise' vacation, having a nontraditional Christmas. Black Sand Beach was the most precious place. I have recently heard that it has since been destroyed by the creeping lava of Kilauea volcano; some places truly exist only in our memories."

Kathryn Davy
Oakland, California

FIG. 7-16b. Kathryn Davy, 10½" x 7½".

The Fabric Postcard

Kathryn Davy's fabric postcard is, like the mock-up in Fig. 5-10, not sewn; instead the fabrics have been adhered with glue stick and double-sided facings. Kathryn chose these methods not only for speed, but also for the type of edge that results. The fabrics she used for the ocean waves are particularly expressive due to their intensity and foamy quality. You can almost hear the bubbles sizzling!

FIG. 7-17a. "Wild Roses Adorn an Old Weathered Shed."

The Picture/Postcard

"The picture is reminiscent of coastal images and our years living in Eureka, California. The postcard was sent to us by an old friend in San Francisco, who enjoys the outdoors as much as we do. Creating a small picture in fabric is like writing haiku poetry – a brief wording to express a large concept or thought."

Betty Schoenhals
Ashland, Oregon

FIG. 7-17b. Betty Schoenhals, 8⅞" x 6½".

The Fabric Postcard

Because of the scale of the floral print fabrics, the wild roses seem capable of completely enveloping the deserted building in Betty Schoenhals' fabric postcard! Many of the fabrics she has chosen have a dusty quality – evoking the weathered surface of splintery boards and the rustling of dry grasses. The deliberately ragged edges of some of the shapes are consistent with that theme; the gradation of tints in her pink border echo that of the postcard.

FIG. 7-18a. Santo ku-ji Temple. Tottori Prefecture: Misasa Hot Springs; Shimane. Photo: Hisako Okawara.

The Picture/Postcard

"This picture was taken in November of 1991, when I took a trip with my brother and sister and their families for the celebration of my brother's sixtieth birthday. In Japan, a sixtieth birthday is a very special celebration, called Kanreki. On that occasion, the honored person is presented with special red clothing."

Hisako Okawara
Hyogo, Japan

FIG. 7-18b. Hisako Okawara, 6⅞" x 5".

The Fabric Postcard

A real understanding of the corresponding value relationships between the photograph and the fabric version is present in Hisako Okawara's work. The natural elements are described simply, while the temple itself is much more specific. The brown and gold plaid works very well as an architectural suggestion, and the tiny brown and white checked fabric perfectly represents the grill-work in the red-orange roof gable.

a coral island Okinawa (photographs by Junkō Hirai)

FIG. 7-19a. A Coral Island. The Seascape in the Evening; Okinawa. Postcard/Photo: Junko Hirai.

The Picture/Postcard

"My fabric postcard became very different from the actual postcard. But I really like my piece; I think the sea creates many moods and feelings...more than the universe."

Junko Nakajima
Tokyo, Japan

FIG. 7-19b. Junko Nakajima, 7¾" x 5⅞".

The Fabric Postcard

Here, we see kimono fabrics with embossed textural patterns reminiscent of the motion of water used to express distant light sparkling on the waves. Junko Nakajima's fabric postcard is an elegantly-styled and well-crafted seascape.

FIG. 7-20a. Hikawa-jinja; Tokyo, Japan. Photo: Noriko Koyama.

The Picture/Postcard

"One day when I was taking a walk at a shrine near my place, I saw a big tree. I remembered that C.W. Nicole said, 'Trees give me all the answers when I hug them.' This is a summer's greeting card."

Noriko Koyama
Tokyo, Japan

FIG. 7-20b. Noriko Koyama, 8½" x 5⅞".

The Fabric Postcard

The unusual perspective of Noriko Koyama's photograph is faithfully echoed in her fabric composition. The tree looms above us, with its bark nicely expressed with a black-and-brown patterned cloth, and the sunlight flashing through its foliage – just as it does in the photo.

"...with beauty all around me, I walk."
–Our Navajo Night Chant

"I am indeed its child. Absolutely, I am Earth's child."
–Our Navajo Song of the Earth

Remember the Pungent Juniper...
Feel the gentle power of beauty...
Remember the purity and strength here...
This sacred place of our People.
–Adapted from the monument overlooking Spider Rock

FIG. 7-21a. Spider Rock; Canyon de Chelly, Arizona. Photo: Jeanne Creighton.

The Picture/Postcard

"This place is so spiritual – Navajo still farm the canyon floor, so access is limited. I like that – keeping the sacred place sacred."

Jeanne Creighton
Denver, Colorado

FIG. 7-21b. Jeanne Creighton, 5½" x 7½".

The Fabric Postcard

Here Jeanne Creighton focuses her attention on clusters of vegetation, little puffs of drifting clouds, linear grooves on the canyon floor – all stated with an eye toward emphasizing the textural patterns of natural forms rather than strict duplications of color and composition. Several of her fabrics are from the Pilgrim/Roy Collection®.

FIG. 7-22a. "La Tour Eiffel la nuit." Postcard/Photo: DeSazo-Rapho.

The Picture/Postcard

"We've made Paris! It's nice to be spending a while in one place, but the country was so much prettier. Saw the Eiffel Tower and Versailles yesterday. Today we go to Notre Dame."

Mabry Benson
Kensington, California

FIG. 7-22b. Mabry Benson, 5½" x 8⅛".

The Fabric Postcard

The Eiffel Tower is illuminated against the night sky in Mabry Benson's piece. Interestingly, the structural ironwork patterns of the tower are surprisingly convincing expressed by sparkling stylized botanical prints! A reflection of patterns of light shimmers in the darkness on the pavement below.

FIG. 7-23a. Barcelona, Spain. Photo: Shigeki Miyatani.

The Picture/Postcard

"This picture was taken by my husband, about twenty years ago. I'm very interested in this photograph – it also became the inspiration for an oil painting."

Machiko Miyatani
Hyogo, Japan

FIG. 7-23b. Machiko Miyatani, 6¼" x 8⅝".

The Fabric Postcard

Machiko Miyatani used tiny amounts of drawing to provide some details. Her piece is exemplary, not only in its faithfulness to the original photograph, but also in its use of the content of patterned fabric to state the architectural qualities of shutters, roof tops, shadowy walls, and stone walkways. The textural pattern used for the building at the left side is particularly expressive of the surface of an ancient wall.

It may be tempting to ask yourself how you would have interpreted any one of the photo sources; there are, of course, many different ways that each one could be translated. Each quiltmaker addressed and solved the design problems inherent in a particular idea; their tools were humor, sentiment, honesty, inventiveness, and a mixture of conscious and/or intuitive use of design vocabulary.

Perhaps one of the most intriguing aspects is the degree to which patterned fabrics can acquire literal content and pictorial voices within the context of the cloth picture – so that prints which in a larger quilt might be characterized as Victorian, Persian, brocade-like, Art Deco, or homespun can, in the right environment, articulate the glass canyons of New York City, mortared blocks of granite, furrowed sandy beaches, farm fields, tile roofs, or weathered boards.

A fabric postcard is simply a vehicle that motivates sincere looking – both outward and inward – that requires selecting an image that has meaning and then developing that image as directly as possible. We all view the world from our own vantage point and love it for different reasons. Whether our work is 5" x 7" or 5' x 7', its content is best expressed and perceived when there is an apparent passion for – and attachment to – the subject.

If these fabric postcards speak at all, it is because the people who made them knew what they were talking about – and they spoke from the heart.

PENNED AND POSTMARKED: The Reverse Side

Designing the reverse side of a fabric postcard can be just as challenging as creating the front. Drawn and written elements, plus fabric collage and appliqué will be useful in accomplishing the basic details found on postcard backs, including (1) the stamp, (2) the postmark, (3) the cancellation mark, (4) the descriptive sentence, (5) the address, (6) postal information such as Air Mail stickers, and (7) the message.

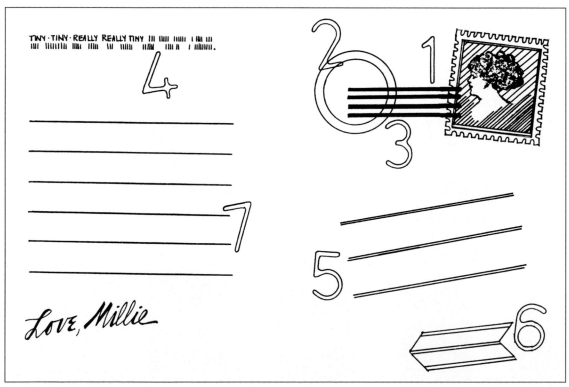

FIG. 8-1. Back details.

The cotton fabric for the back of your postcard may be white, a white-on-white print, or anything else you think appropriate – stiffened to replicate a card-like firmness by your applying to the underside of the backing fabric the sturdiest and thickest iron-on facing you can find. It is very helpful to make two of these faced pieces; one that will become the actual postcard back and one, made of the same fabric, on which you can practice various writing styles and try out different pens.

The raw-edged size of the back surface will be exactly the same as the raw-edged size of the front; here, as with the front, it is important to remember not to place any important details (such as the last three letters of the addressee's name) in the outer ⅜" – ½" of any edge, where they might look crowded or even be concealed when you attach and turn the binding that will finish the edges of your postcard.

Experimenting with a complete layout on a piece of paper cut to size will be helpful in composing the content, the scale of the writing, the size of the stamp, etc.

FABRIC STAMPS:
The pictorial content of your postage stamp can include any imagery that seems illustrative and convincing – look for florals, foliage, tiny buildings, and other stamp-like themes you can extract from patterned yardage. There are even fabrics printed with replicas of actual or imaginary postage stamps! Be sure to relate the size of your fabric stamp and the scale of its image to the size of your fabric postcard.

FIG. 8-2. (Top row, l – r): Stamp-theme fabrics; "perforations" can be drawn at the edge of the shape or cut with pinking shears. The lighthouse and airplane fabric suggest institutional and governmental content; the borders and other details were drawn with black and silver pens. (Bottom row, l – r): Variations on an Abraham Lincoln rubber stamp – which Mabry Benson found in a rubber stamp store that had many kinds of "postal detail" stamps – imprinted onto small pieces of cloth with drawn borders, frames, and "engraving" patterns added for embellishment and authenticity.

FIG. 8-3. Pictorial fabrics that seem to have been designed specifically for use as commemorative postage stamps – florals and other botanicals, pictorials and graphic designs.

FIG. 8-4. It is great fun when you can find fabric that nearly duplicates the design and coloration of postage stamps currently in use.

The stamps in Figures 8-5 through 8-9, taken from the reverse sides of fabric post-cards, show further examples of fabrics having stamp-like imagery and demonstrate different options for edgings and for attaching the stamp.

Your fabric stamp can be machine or hand-sewn to the postcard back. If you want to attach it by means of hand-appliqué, do so *before* you iron the heavy facing to the back fabric. Fabric stamps can also be adhered to a double-sided facing, edged with pointed or scalloped pinking shears or a wavy-edged cutting wheel, and ironed into place.

POSTAL DETAILS:
Whether you prefer black or colored ink pens (or silver, which works nicely for embell-ishing and decorating fabric stamps), try different pens on your faced practice fabric, to see which work best. Some pens may blur on certain fabrics and be perfectly sharp and clear on others (Fig. 8-10).

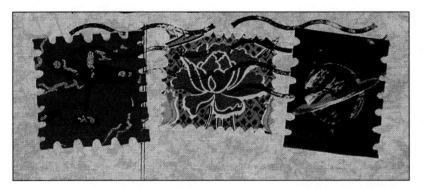

FIG. 8-5. Yachiyo Monarrez edged her stamps to suggest the half-cir-cles of the perforations.

FIG. 8-6 (above). Toshiko Okage's stamp fabric could have been designed as a Winter Olympics Commerora-tive.

FIG. 8-7 (left). Fukiko Hayase used a fabric that looks like a detail from a page in an atlas, focusing on geography as stamps often do!

FIG. 8-8 (right). Tetsuko Chōsho's little landscape is par-ticularly effective with the post-mark superimposed.

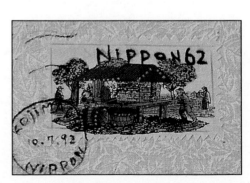

Written and drawn elements you may want to include will be the country of origin and the denomination of the stamp, as well as postmarks and cancellation marks. Often, at the top left corner on the back of a postcard, there is a sentence or two which describes, in glowing terminology, interesting features of the locale pictured on the front.

IF YOU WISH TO INCLUDE THIS DETAIL, YOU WILL WANT TO PRACTICE VERY TINY AND VERY REGULAR CAPITAL LETTER PRINTING — BOTH ON PAPER AND ON YOUR EXPERIMENTATION PIECE OF FACED FABRIC.

FIG. 8-9. Top row (left to right): Hisako Okawara's appliquéd stamp celebrates the Phillipines; Machiko Miyatani used an embroidered stamp; Sachie Koshimura hand-appliquéd the irregular edges of her stamp. Bottom row (left to right): Mabry Benson rubber stamped directly onto her postcard back, while Rumi Shikata, who used the same fabric as Sachie Koshimura, folded her edges under and attached the stamp with a row of machine stitches that frame the stamp.

FIG. 8-10. Know how your pen reacts with your particular fabric.

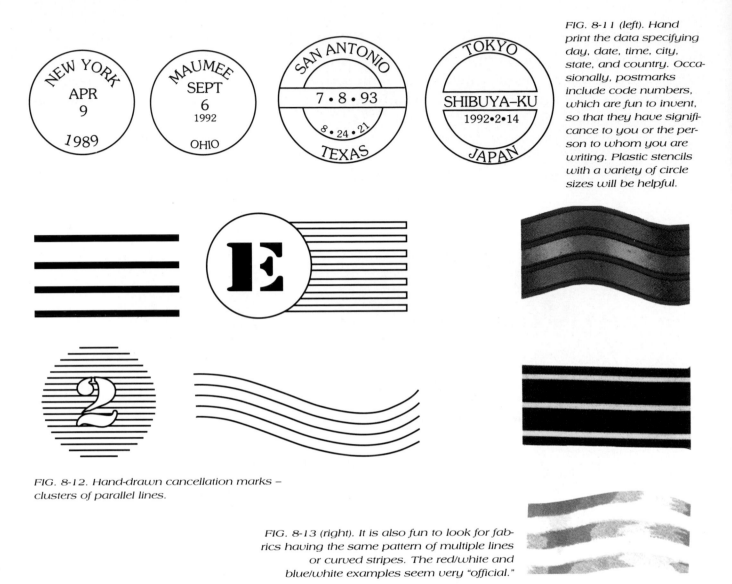

FIG. 8-11 (left). Hand print the data specifying day, date, time, city, state, and country. Occasionally, postmarks include code numbers, which are fun to invent, so that they have significance to you or the person to whom you are writing. Plastic stencils with a variety of circle sizes will be helpful.

FIG. 8-12. Hand-drawn cancellation marks – clusters of parallel lines.

FIG. 8-13 (right). It is also fun to look for fabrics having the same pattern of multiple lines or curved stripes. The red/white and blue/white examples seem very "official."

THE ADDRESS:

You can print, write in your usual script, or write in an embellished calligraphic style. As a practical consideration, make sure that the writing style and the scale will fit within the address area of the postcard back. Doing a practice layout on paper will assure you that the address won't be too big for the space.

POSTAL EMBELLISHMENTS:

You may want to reserve some space in the address area for decorative details that will heighten the "official" quality of the postcard.

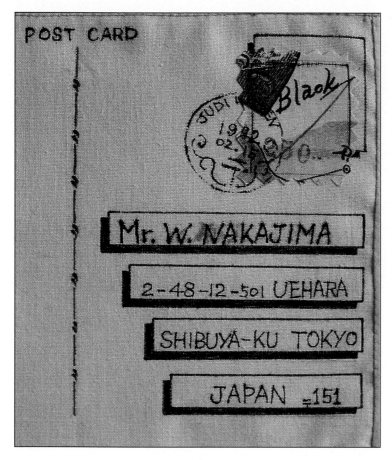

FIG. 8-14. Junko Nakajima addressed this postcard in a very graphic fashion.

FIG. 8-15. Postal embellishments may include rubber stamps that provide humor or authenticity via postal vocabulary, striped fabric for Air Mail stickers, etc.

FIG. 8-16. A postcard with an added embellishment, not having connection to postal references, but to the regional features of the locale of the picture on the front. A bag of salt sewn to the back of a Salton Sea postcard suggests the possibility of attaching a meaningful remembrance.

THE MESSAGE:

Originally, there was no space reserved on a postcard for even a brief message; you simply addressed the back and sent the picture through the mail. However, people could not resist writing little messages on the front. Later, the backs were divided into message and address halves.

The most eloquent message is, of course, the one that only you can send – the one that reveals and reflects your personality. Antique picture postcards give us the opportunity to compare geographical and architectural subjects as they were presented in 1900 or 1940, in contrast to our own time; and if they were mailed, we were also able to observe writing styles and read messages that had meaning for the writer and the recipient, but may be totally puzzling to us. It is, admittedly, reading someone else's mail – something your grandmother told you never to do! Still, there are fascinating qualities of distance and innocence in those messages from another time, qualities which remind us to give thought to the wording and the meaning of the message we write on a fabric postcard.

A certain gentility is revealed, for instance, in the comment written in now-faded brown ink across the bottom front edge of a 1900's postcard picturing the George Bernard Shaw Botanical Gardens in St. Louis, Missouri – "G.B. Shaw; how we miss you." Ninety years from now, a vintage postcard commemorating the opening of The Rock and Roll Museum, with a message written in flourescent ink saying, "Mick Jagger – later, Dude!" might seem just as quaint. Even ten years from now, the message you write on your fabric postcard will speak for you about your life and times.

Because of the small space alloted, postcard messages are of necessity brief; however they can still be intriguing. They are sometimes predictable – "Having a wonderful time"; but they can also be enigmatic – "Arrived at 8:30 AM, left at 9:30 AM" (...*not* having a wonderful time?). They can be mysterious – "Theodore will bring the violin on Wednesday" (...who *was* Theodore and *why* was he bringing the violin?). Messages can be romantic or silly or fictitious. They can describe daily life and document memorable events, as in Barbara Friedman's message on the back of her Oakland Bay Bridge postcard (p. 60) – "...Rented a car and drove to New Pieces Gallery in Berkeley. Bought new fabric! Saw nude people on a street corner! What a weekend!"

A message can be touched with humor, or with the kind of friendly teasing that Dena Bliss used in the message on her Yucatan postcard on page 81 – "We're having a great time. You *wouldn't* like it." Humor can also be based on incidental knowledge shared by the writer and the person to whom he/she is writing. Whether the joke was intentional or unintentional, the message written on the front of the Detroit Waterworks postcard below is even more endearing if you know that there is a town in Michigan called Bad Axe.

If the picture side of your fabric postcard represents your artistic nature, the message side reflects your literary self; both sides deserve the same thoughtful planning. Using imagination, humor, attention to detail, and content inspired by personal references and shared experiences, you can make the back as appealing as the front.

FIG. 8-17. Waterworks Park.

HANDLE WITH CARE: Finishing and Displaying

The process of finishing a fabric postcard is almost the same as attaching the binding that joins the edges of the front and back layers of a larger quilt, except that there is no batting layer in between. First, position the front and back of your fabric postcard, *wrong sides together*, perfectly aligned. Make sure they are exactly the same size; trim, if necessary.

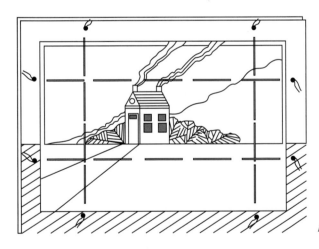

FIG. 9-1. Basting the layers together.

You'll need to remember that the pieced and/or appliquéd front will be more stretchy and flexible than the faced back; in order to avoid ending up with bulges on the front, it's a good idea to baste through both layers, smoothing the front outward toward the edges. Then, you can re-trim, if necessary, before you machine stitch the binding.

With a one inch or slightly wider binding strip of white or other border fabric placed face down and parallel to the edge of the postcard front, machine stitch ¼" in from the

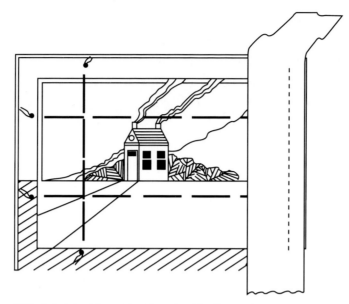

FIG. 9-2. Machine attaching the binding strips.

raw edge, catching the front, the back, and the binding layers. In the Chapter 7 examples, you will see that some bindings have mitered corners while others are squared; either is fine.

Finally, turn the binding to the back of the fabric postcard, fold it crisply in half to a ¼" width and invisibly hand stitch to the backing layer to finish the edge (Fig. 9-3).

Another finishing method omits the element of a bordered or framed edge, taking into consideration that some postcard pictures are not printed with a border. If this is the

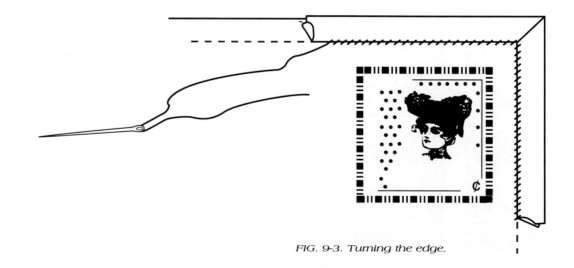

FIG. 9-3. Turning the edge.

case, you should initially make the facing for your postcard back ¼" smaller on all sides so that the seam allowance will be unfaced fabric. Then, position the front and back layers *right sides together*; after basting, machine-stitch ¼" from the raw edge around three sides only. Turn right side out, tuck the unsewn edges inward, and hand-stitch to close the fourth side. This method was used in the pictures shown in Figs. 7-4b, 7-11b, 7-17b, and 7-22b.

Only one final decision remains: a choice of several ways to display something that is this tiny and has two sides, both of which are meant to be seen. Even though it did not take ten months to make, your fabric postcard deserves to be "handled with care." If you just casually place it on your coffee table, you risk the possibility that someone will mistake it for a very artfully done coaster...and rest a glass of lemonade on it!

You'll also want to avoid using push-pins and other sharp instruments. For a single fabric postcard, a nice solution is to display it in a plexi-glass frame or a "glass sandwich" that allows both sides to be viewed. A collection of several fabric postcards can be stored in hand-made cloth boxes or albums; or if you wish to reveal the contents and invite browsing, place them in clear acetate envelopes or portfolios. Another possibility is to tie a group of fabric postcards together in a bundle, secured with a beautiful piece of ribbon (Fig. 9-4). Just untie the ribbon...and take a trip around the world!

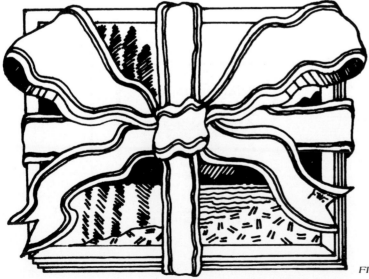

FIG. 9-4. Postcards tied together in a bundle.

P.S.

Looking is basic to the making of Art – whether that Art is a beautifully composed descriptive paragraph, a literal or abstract painting, or a pictorial or geometric quilt. If in looking and observing we truly perceive the relationships that exist within a source of inspiration, we are then able to re-create them or choose to grant them added emphasis by transforming or enhancing them. If we perceive the relationships that exist in a work-in-progress, we are able to refine them.

Although this book focuses on a very specific object – a fabric postcard – its underlying message suggests the importance of looking and responding to visual information, no matter what the source or what form that response assumes, expressing what you have to say as eloquently as possible.

While it does challenge you to look for and really see the visual relationships that are the foundation of any sound composition, making a fabric postcard can be much more than an exercise in duplicating a photographic image in cloth. It can also be a process that generates fresh approaches to the designing of geometric, pictorial, and abstract quilts, no matter what their scale. It allows you to think about the properties and potentials of patterned fabric in ways you may not have considered before and encourages you to make critical choices, to build fluency in the use of the principles of color and design, and, most importantly, to look inside yourself, to recall and interpret a locale you love and care about – a time you can't forget!

The reward is that, in the process, you will create a beautiful little cloth object that expresses a sense of place and a sense of yourself, and at the same time says:

"…wish you were here."

POSTCARD CREDITS

Postcards from the collection of the author, chapters 4, 5, 6, and 8

Fig. 4-1. Bathing Ghat: Howrah Bridge. No reference available.

Fig. 4-2. "A Typical Park in California." M. Rieder, Publ. Los Angeles, California. No. 3186 Made in Germany.

Fig. 4-3. "A Little Bit of Heaven," Nantucket, Mass. B 1236, Copyright by H. Marshall Gardener; Nantucket, Mass.

Fig. 4-4. New Post Office and Federal Building; Los Angeles, California. Published by Van Noy Interstate Company.

Fig. 5-7. Fairmont Hotel after the Fire and Earthquake; San Francisco, California. H.S. Crocker Co., San Francisco and Sacramento (from Sonya Lee Barrington)

Fig. 5-8. Michigan Avenue; Albion, Michigan. E.C. Kropp Co., Milwaukee (Domestic, Canada, G. Britain, Germany: one cent...Foreign: two cents.)

Fig. 5-9. "Lake in Allen Park," Augusta, Georgia. T American Art A-58640 1¢

Fig. 6-1. (Contemporary) "The Fashion Center of Tokyo, Omote-Sandō in Autumn." 130 Published by NBC (Nippon Beauty Colour) Inc. Japan NBC®

Fig. 6-2. "Flowers and Palms at Central Park"; Pasadena, CA. Published by Van Noy Interstate Company

Fig. 8-16. Deseret Book Company; Salt Lake City, Utah. Southern Pacific Lines. Genuine Curteich-Chicago C.T. Art-Color-tone Postcard. (Reg. U.S. Pat. Off.) Postage, if salt bag attached with message: 3¢; without message: 1½¢. (From Yvonne Porcella.)

Fig. 8-17. Raphael Tuck & Sons' Postcard Series No. 2139, "Detroit, Mich." Art Publishers to their Majesties the King and Queen.

Contemporary Postcard Sources illustrated in Chapter 7

Fig. 7-2a. Impact Photo Graphics: 4961 Windplay Drive; El Dorado Hills, California 95762. ©Impact, Inc. 1978.

Fig. 7-3a. Postcard; Hannya-ji; Nara, Japan. No further reference available.

Fig. 7-4a. Postcard: ©1980-1983. Christo/C.V.J. Corporation.

Fig. 7-6a. Bookplate catalog: Berliner and McGinnis; Nevada City, California 95959. #4050 Cathedral. No longer in business.

Fig. 7-11a. ©1982 FVN Corporation: P.O. Box 68; Redcrest, California 95569 B11488 Kolar View; Oakland, California.

Fig. 7-14a. Worldwide Distributors Ltd. Honolulu. Curteichcolor® 3-D Natural Color Repro's (Reg. U.S. Pat. Off.) D-19704.

Fig. 7-16a. A Salmon Cameracolour® Postcard, printed in England. "Salthouse Church": 2-29-03-17. J. Salmon Ltd. Seven Oaks, Kent.

Fig. 7-18a. ©Eastman Postcards West GE-2266. No other reference available.

Fig. 7-20a. Postcard: Okinawa. No further reference available.

Fig. 7-23a. AGEP Line Collection-Prestige Editions. ©AGEP Marseille Imprimé en France. Ref.: 50 000 129 DeSazo-Rapho.

INDEX:
The Quiltmakers

CUSTOM FABRIC SOURCES

DYEING TO QUILT and
SIMPLY MARBELOUS
Sonya Lee Barrington
837 47th Ave.
San Francisco, CA 94121

KATIE'S COLLECTIONS
Katie Pasquini-Masopust
230 Rancho Alegre Rd.
Santa Fe, NM 87505

MARBELED FABRICS AND ACCESSORIES
Marjorie Bevis
325 4th St.
Petaluma, CA 94952

SHADES, INC.
The Nunn Complex; Studio "O"
585 Cobb Pkwy, S.
Marietta, GA 30062

Mickey Lawler's SKYDYES
83 Richmond Lane
W. Hartford, CT 06117

American Quilter's Society

dedicated to publishing books for today's quilters

The following AQS publications are currently available:

- **Adapting Architectural Details for Quilts**, Carol Wagner, #2282: AQS, 1991, 88 pages, softbound, $12.95
- **American Beauties: Rose & Tulip Quilts**, Gwen Marston & Joe Cunningham, #1907: AQS, 1988, 96 pages, softbound, $14.95
- **America's Pictorial Quilts**, Caron L. Mosey, #1662: AQS, 1985, 112 pages, hardbound, $19.95
- **Applique Designs: My Mother Taught Me to Sew**, Faye Anderson, #2121: AQS, 1990, 80 pages, softbound, $12.95
- **Arkansas Quilts: Arkansas Warmth**, Arkansas Quilter's Guild, Inc., #1908: AQS, 1987, 144 pages, hardbound, $24.95
- **The Art of Hand Applique**, Laura Lee Fritz, #2122: AQS, 1990, 80 pages, softbound, $14.95
- **...Ask Helen More About Quilting Designs**, Helen Squire, #2099: AQS, 1990, 54 pages, 17 x 11, spiral-bound, $14.95
- **Award-Winning Quilts & Their Makers: Vol. I, The Best of AQS Shows – 1985-1987**, #2207: AQS, 1991, 232 pages, softbound, $24.95
- **Award-Winning Quilts & Their Makers: Vol. II, The Best of AQS Shows – 1988-1989**, #2354: AQS, 1992, 176 pages, softbound, $24.95
- **Award-Winning Quilts & Their Makers: Vol. III, The Best of AQS Shows – 1990-1991**, #3425: AQS, 1993, 180 pages, softbound, $24.95
- **Classic Basket Quilts**, Elizabeth Porter & Marianne Fons, #2208: AQS, 1991, 128 pages, softbound, $16.95
- **A Collection of Favorite Quilts**, Judy Florence, #2119: AQS, 1990, 136 pages, softbound, $18.95
- **Creative Machine Art**, Sharee Dawn Roberts, #2355: AQS, 1992, 142 pages, 9 x 9, softbound, $24.95
- **Dear Helen, Can You Tell Me?...all about quilting designs**, Helen Squire, #1820: AQS, 1987, 51 pages, 17 x 11, spiral-bound, $12.95
- **Dye Painting!**, Ann Johnston, #3399: AQS, 1992, 88 pages, softbound, $19.95
- **Dyeing & Overdyeing of Cotton Fabrics**, Judy Mercer Tescher, #2030: AQS, 1990, 54 pages, softbound, $9.95
- **Encyclopedia of Pieced Quilt Patterns**, compiled by Barbara Brackman, #3468: AQS, 1993, 552 pages, hardbound, $34.95
- **Flavor Quilts for Kids to Make: Complete Instructions for Teaching Children to Dye, Decorate & Sew Quilts**, Jennifer Amor #2356: AQS, 1991, 120 pages, softbound, $12.95
- **From Basics to Binding: A Complete Guide to Making Quilts**, Karen Kay Buckley, #2381: AQS, 1992, 160 pages, softbound, $16.95
- **Fun & Fancy Machine Quiltmaking**, Lois Smith, #1982: AQS, 1989, 144 pages, softbound, $19.95
- **Gallery of American Quilts 1830-1991: Book III**, #3421: AQS, 1992, 128 pages, softbound, $19.95
- **The Grand Finale: A Quilter's Guide to Finishing Projects**, Linda Denner, #1924: AQS, 1988, 96 pages, softbound, $14.95
- **Heirloom Miniatures**, Tina M. Gravatt, #2097: AQS, 1990, 64 pages, softbound, $9.95
- **Infinite Stars**, Gayle Bong, #2283: AQS, 1992, 72 pages, softbound, $12.95
- **Jacobean Appliqué: Book I, "Exotica,"** Patricia B. Campbell & Mimi Ayars, Ph.D, #3784: AQS, 1993, 160 pages, softbound, $18.95
- **The Ins and Outs: Perfecting the Quilting Stitch**, Patricia J. Morris, #2120: AQS, 1990, 96 pages, softbound, $9.95
- **Irish Chain Quilts: A Workbook of Irish Chains & Related Patterns**, Joyce B. Peaden, #1906: AQS, 1988, 96 pages, softbound, $14.95
- **The Log Cabin Returns to Kentucky: Quilts from the Pilgrim/Roy Collection**, Gerald Roy and Paul Pilgrim, #3329: AQS, 1992, 36 pages, 9 x 7, softbound, $12.95
- **Marbling Fabrics for Quilts: A Guide for Learning & Teaching**, Kathy Fawcett & Carol Shoaf, #2206: AQS, 1991, 72 pages, softbound, $12.95
- **More Projects and Patterns: A Second Collection of Favorite Quilts**, Judy Florence, #3330: AQS, 1992, 152 pages, softbound, $18.95
- **Nancy Crow: Quilts and Influences**, Nancy Crow, #1981: AQS, 1990, 256 pages, 9 x 12, hardcover, $29.95
- **Nancy Crow: Work in Transition**, Nancy Crow, #3331: AQS, 1992, 32 pages, 9 x 10, softbound, $12.95
- **New Jersey Quilts – 1777 to 1950: Contributions to an American Tradition**, The Heritage Quilt Project of New Jersey; text by Rachel Cochran, Rita Erickson, Natalie Hart & Barbara Schaffer, #3332: AQS, 1992, 256 pages, softbound, $29.95
- **No Dragons on My Quilt**, Jean Ray Laury with Ritva Laury & Lizabeth Laury, #2153: AQS, 1990, 52 pages, hardcover, $12.95
- **Oklahoma Heritage Quilts**, Oklahoma Quilt Heritage Project #2032: AQS, 1990, 144 pages, softbound, $19.95
- **Old Favorites in Miniature**, Tina Gravatt #3469: AQS, 1993, 104 pages, softbound, $15.95
- **Quilt Groups Today: Who They Are, Where They Meet, What They Do, and How to Contact Them; A Complete Guide for 1992-1993**, #3308: AQS, 1992, 336 pages, softbound, $14.95
- **Quilt Registry**, Lynne Fritz, #2380: AQS, 1992, 80 pages, hardbound, $9.95
- **Quilting Patterns from Native American Designs**, Dr. Joyce Mori, #3467: AQS, 1993, 80 pages, softbound, $12.95
- **Quilting with Style: Principles for Great Pattern Design**, Gwen Marston & Joe Cunningham #3470: AQS, 1993, 192 pages, 9 x 12, hardbound, $24.95
- **Quiltmaker's Guide: Basics & Beyond**, Carol Doak, #2284: AQS, 1992, 208 pages, softbound, $19.95
- **Quilts: Old & New, A Similar View**, Paul D. Pilgrim and Gerald E. Roy, #3715: AQS, 1993, 40 pages, softbound, $12.95
- **Quilts: The Permanent Collection – MAQS**, #2257: AQS, 1991, 100 pages, 10 x 6½, softbound, $9.95
- **Seasons of the Heart & Home: Quilts for a Winter's Day**, Jan Patek, #3796: AQS, 1993, 160 pages, softbound, $18.95
- **Seasons of the Heart & Home: Quilts for Summer Days**, Jan Patek, #3761: AQS, 1993, 160 pages, softbound, $18.95
- **Sensational Scrap Quilts**, Darra Duffy Williamson, #2357: AQS, 1992, 152 pages, softbound, $24.95
- **Sets & Borders**, Gwen Marston & Joe Cunningham, #1821: AQS, 1987, 104 pages, softbound, $14.95
- **Show Me Helen...How to Use Quilting Designs**, Helen Squire, #3375: AQS, 1993, 155 pages, softbound, $15.95
- **Somewhere in Between: Quilts and Quilters of Illinois**, Rita Barrow Barber, #1790: AQS, 1986, 78 pages, softbound, $14.95
- **Spike & Zola: Patterns for Laughter...and Appliqué, Painting, or Stenciling**, Donna F. Collins, #3794: AQS, 1993, 72 pages, softbound, $9.95
- **Stenciled Quilts for Christmas**, Marie Monteith Sturmer, #2098: AQS, 1990, 104 pages, softbound, $14.95
- **A Treasury of Quilting Designs**, Linda Goodmon Emery, #2029: AQS, 1990, 80 pages, 14 x 11, spiral-bound, $14.95
- **Wonderful Wearables: A Celebration of Creative Clothing**, Virginia Avery, #2286: AQS, 1991, 184 pages, softbound, $24.95

These books can be found in local bookstores and quilt shops. If you are unable to locate a title in your area, you can order by mail from AQS, P.O. Box 3290, Paducah, KY 42002-3290. Please add $1 for the first book and 40¢ for each additional one to cover postage and handling. (International orders please add $1.50 for the first book and $1 for each additional one.)

FABRIC POSTCARDS

LANDMARKS & LANDSCAPES • MONUMENTS & MEADOWS

JUDI WARREN

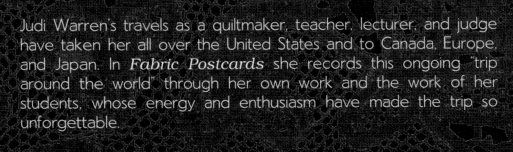

Making a fabric postcard is really all about looking at, recording, and communicating personal insights and themes. This book will make you want to create your own small cloth object that expresses a sense of place and a sense of yourself, and at the same time says:

"...wish you were here."

Judi Warren's travels as a quiltmaker, teacher, lecturer, and judge have taken her all over the United States and to Canada, Europe, and Japan. In *Fabric Postcards* she records this ongoing "trip around the world" through her own work and the work of her students, whose energy and enthusiasm have made the trip so unforgettable.

Judi received her B.S. in art education from Eastern Michigan University and an M.F.A. from Bowling Green State University in Ohio. Her professional career has been spent teaching art to elementary school children, to college-level drawing and design foundations students, and to quiltmakers. Her popular workshops encourage exploration and discovery and challenge students to express their own dreams and memories in their quilts. Judi is a frequent participant in gallery shows and Quilt National exhibitions, and her works are in public and private collections in Michigan, Ohio, California, Japan, and Australia.

American Quilter's Society

P. O. Box 3290 • Paducah, KY 42002-3290
US$22.95

DESTINOS

VOLUME 1 EPISODIOS 1–26

Third Edition

**VanPatten
Marks
Teschner**